A LOOK AT SPACE SCIENCE

THE PLANETS

BY BERT WILBERFORCE

Gareth Stevens PUBLISHING

CRASHCOURSE

Please visit our website, www.garethstevens.com. For a free color catalog of all our high-quality books, call toll free 1-800-542-2595 or fax 1-877-542-2596.

Library of Congress Cataloging-in-Publication Data
Names: Wilberforce, Bert, author.
Title: The planets / Bert Wilberforce.
Description: New York : Gareth Stevens Publishing, [2021] | Series: A look at space science | Includes bibliographical references and index. | Contents: Our eight planets -- What is a planet? -- The rocky planets -- The gas giants -- The ice giants -- Planetary explorations -- Outside out solar system -- How far from the sun?.
Identifiers: LCCN 2019050743 | ISBN 9781538259207 (library binding) | ISBN 9781538259184 (paperback) | ISBN 9781538259191 | ISBN 9781538259214 (ebook)
Subjects: LCSH: Planets--Juvenile literature.
Classification: LCC QB602 .W55 2021 | DDC 523.4--dc23
LC record available at https://lccn.loc.gov/2019050743

First Edition

Published in 2021 by
Gareth Stevens Publishing
111 East 14th Street, Suite 349
New York, NY 10003

Designer: Sarah Liddell
Editor: Therese Shea

Photo credits: Cover, pp. 1 (main), 9, 11, 13, 21, 23, 25 Vadim Sadovski/Shutterstock.com; background used throughout Zakharchuk/Shutterstock.com; p. 5 Peter Hermes Furian/ Shutterstock.com; p. 7 Johan Swanepoel/Shutterstock.com; p. 15 buradaki/Shutterstock.com; p. 17 Elena11/Shutterstock.com; p. 19 Sittikorn Thongkhaw/Shutterstock.com; p. 27 MPI/ Stringer/Archive Photos/Getty Images; p. 29 Universal History Archive /Contributor/Universal Images Group/Getty Images.

Printed in the United States of America

CPSIA compliance information: Batch #CS20GS: For further information contact Gareth Stevens, New York, New York at 1-800-542-2595.

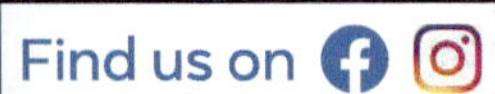

CONTENTS

Words in the glossary appear in **bold** type the first time they are used in the text.

OUR EIGHT PLANETS

Our solar system is made up of our sun, eight planets, and other objects in space that move around the sun. In order from closest to the sun to the farthest, our solar system's planets are Mercury, Venus, Earth, Mars, Jupiter, Saturn, Uranus, and Neptune.

MAKE THE GRADE

You can see the planets Mercury, Venus, Mars, Jupiter, and Saturn from Earth without a **telescope**!

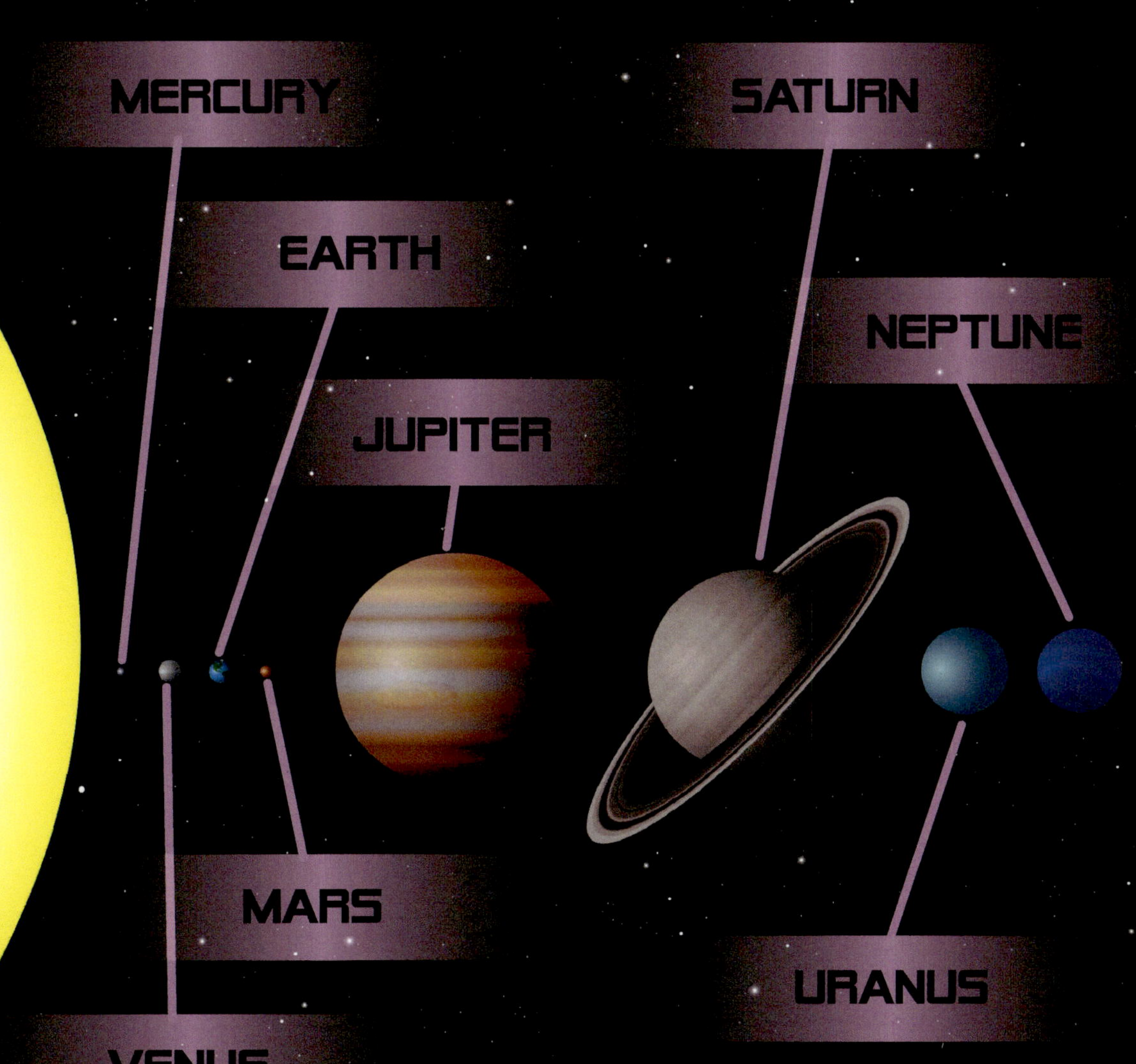

WHAT IS A PLANET?

In 2006, a group of scientists defined, or explained, what a planet is. First, a planet orbits, or goes around, a star. It must be large so its **gravity** is strong enough to pull it into a round shape.

MAKE THE GRADE

A planet can't be a satellite of another planet. A satellite is an object that orbits another space object, like the moon and the man-made machines that orbit Earth.

A planet's gravity must be strong enough to clear objects from its orbit around the sun. Pluto once was called a planet. However, it doesn't clear objects such as rocks from its orbit. That's why it's not called a planet anymore.

MAKE THE GRADE

Pluto and some other large space objects are called dwarf planets. They're like planets in some ways, but can't clear objects from their orbits around the sun.

THE ROCKY PLANETS

The four planets closest to the sun are called rocky planets. They're hard with a rocky **surface.** Mercury is the closest to the sun. It's also the smallest planet. It's less than half Earth's size. It takes about 88 Earth days for it to travel around the sun.

MAKE THE GRADE

Mercury spins slowly. One day on Mercury is about 176 Earth days!

Venus is the next planet from the sun. It's rocky like Mercury. It's about the same size as Earth. Venus is the hottest planet in the solar system. **Temperatures** near its surface can be about 900°F (482°C)!

MAKE THE GRADE

Venus's surface has mountains and **volcanoes**! It may have had water at one time.

Earth is the third planet from the sun. Its average distance from the sun is about 92 **million** miles (150 million km)! It's the only planet in the solar system known to have life. It's also the only planet that has water on its surface.

MAKE THE GRADE

Earth's **atmosphere** has the right mix of gases for us to breathe. The atmosphere also breaks up most space rocks before they crash onto Earth's surface!

Mars is the fourth planet from the sun. It's called the red planet because iron on its surface rusts. This gives the planet a reddish color. Mars has a thin atmosphere that cannot **support** life as we know it.

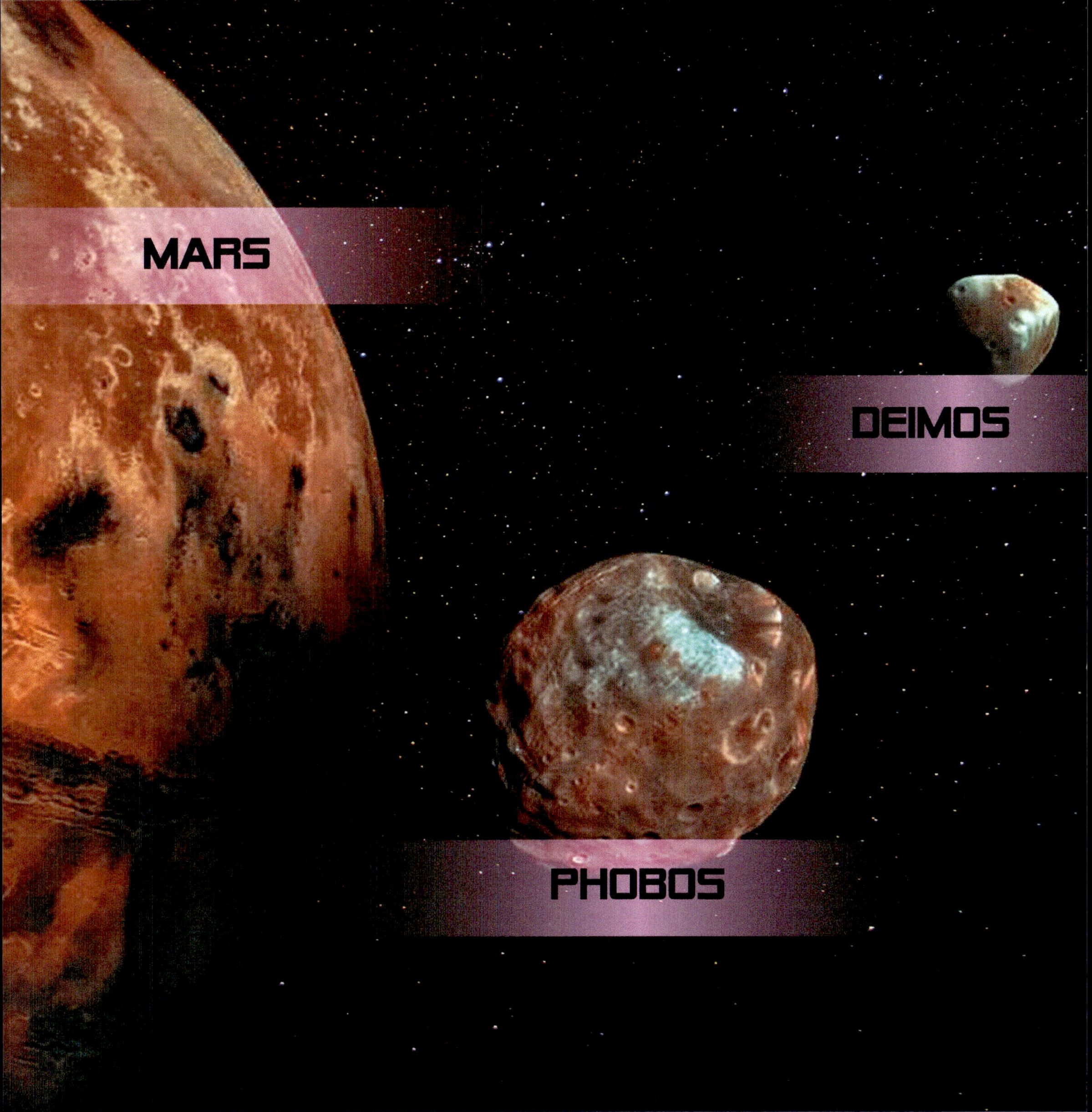

MARS

DEIMOS

PHOBOS

MAKE THE GRADE

Mars has two moons called Phobos and Deimos.

THE GAS GIANTS

Jupiter is the fifth planet from the sun. It's called a gas giant. It doesn't have a solid surface. It's made up mostly of the gases hydrogen and helium. However, it may have a solid core, or center. Jupiter has 79 moons!

GREAT
RED SPOT

MAKE THE GRADE

Jupiter is the largest planet. More than 1,300 Earths could fit inside it. A storm on Jupiter called the Great Red Spot is wider than Earth!

Saturn is the sixth planet from the sun. It's the second largest planet. Like Jupiter, this gas giant is made up mostly of hydrogen and helium. It is circled by a large system of rings, which are made of ice and dust.

MAKE THE GRADE

Saturn has 82 moons! Scientists are studying whether some of Saturn's moons could support life.

THE ICE GIANTS

Uranus is the seventh planet from the sun. One year on Uranus takes 84 Earth years! The planet's blue color comes from the methane gas in its atmosphere. Uranus is called an ice giant because it's mostly made up of icy matter.

MAKE THE GRADE

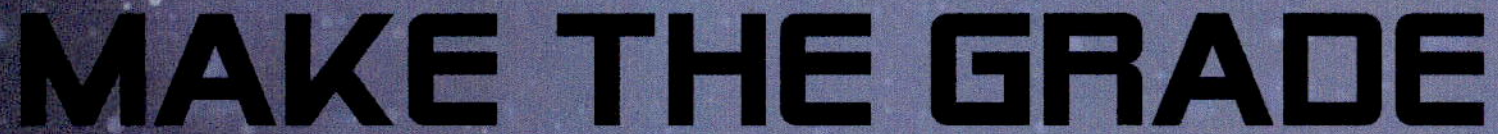

Uranus spins on its side!
Thirteen rings circle it.

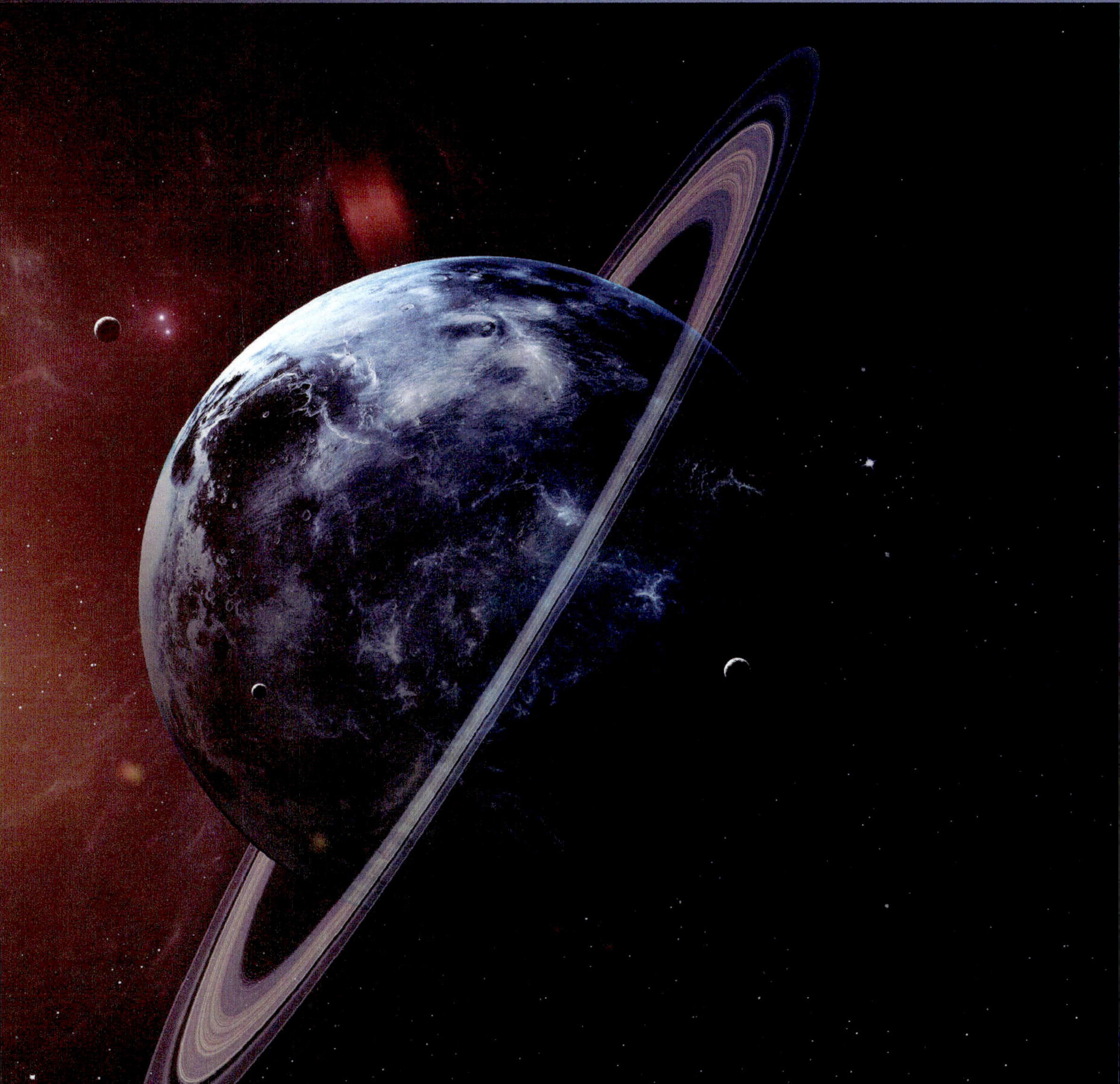

Neptune is the farthest planet from the sun in our solar system. It takes 165 Earth years to orbit the sun. This ice giant is the windiest planet too. Its winds can be faster than 1,200 miles (1,930 km) per hour!

MAKE THE GRADE

Except for Earth, all the planets have names from old Greek and Roman stories. Neptune was the Roman god of the sea.

PLANETARY EXPLORATIONS

Spacecraft have visited every planet in the solar system. Some have landed on the planets. Only one spacecraft has visited Uranus and Neptune. The **NASA** probe Voyager 2 flew by these planets on its way out of the solar system!

MAKE THE GRADE

A probe is an unmanned ship that sends **data** to Earth. Voyager 2 left Earth in 1977 and is still working. It carries a message for any life forms it might meet!

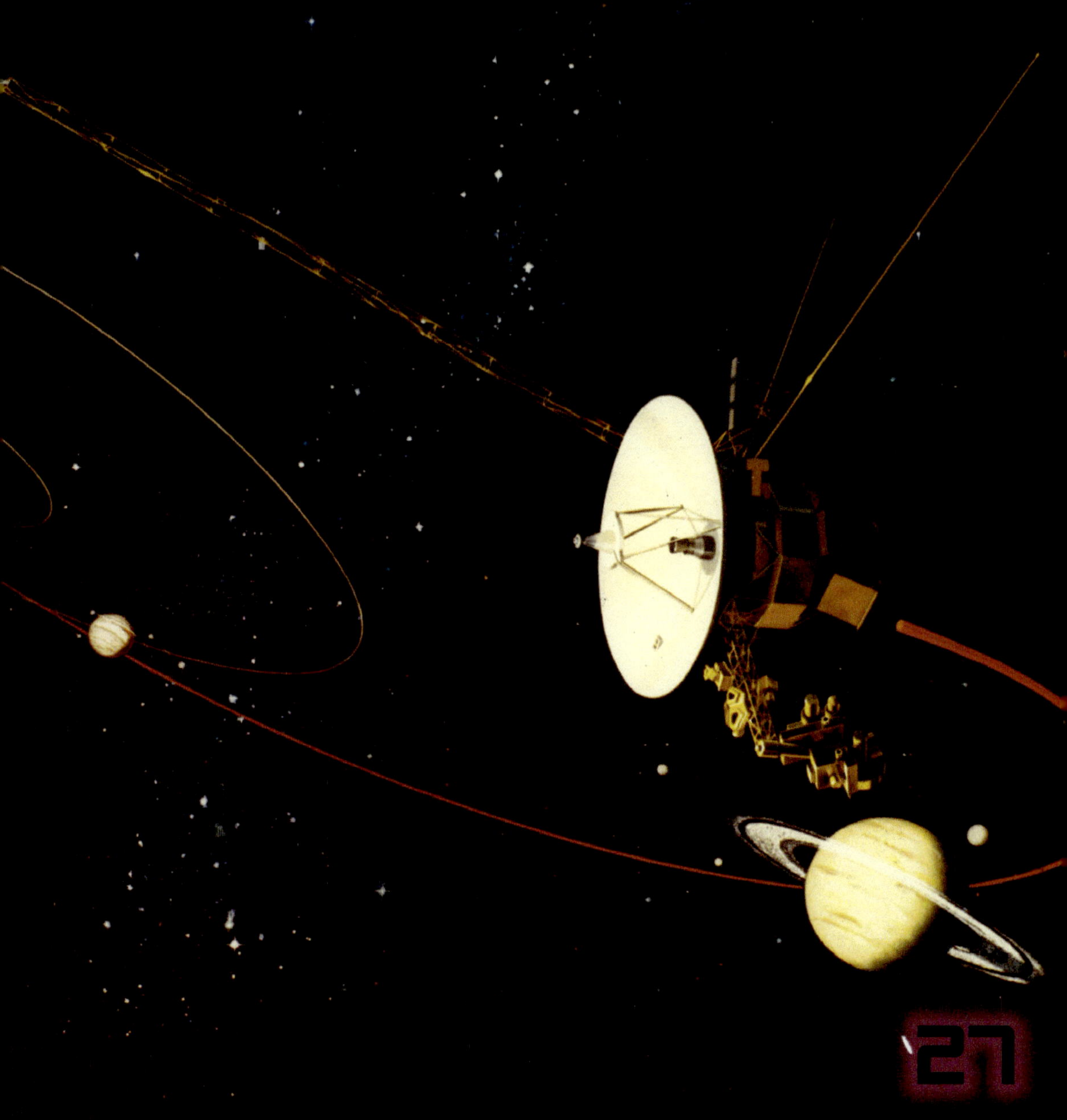

OUTSIDE OUR SOLAR SYSTEM

Planets outside our solar system are called exoplanets. They orbit other stars. Thanks to amazing telescopes, satellites, and other space machines, scientists have found more than 3,700 exoplanets. They're trying to discover if any can support life. There's so much more to learn!

KEPLER-22B

KEPLER-69C

KEPLER-452B

KEPLER-186F

KEPLER-62F

MAKE THE GRADE

NASA's Transiting Exoplanet Survey Satellite (TESS) is looking for exoplanets, like the ones above.

HOW FAR FROM THE SUN?

PLANET	AVERAGE DISTANCE FROM THE SUN (ROUNDED)
Mercury	36,000,000 miles (58,000,000 km)
Venus	67,000,000 miles (108,000,000 km)
Earth	93,000,000 miles (150,000,000 km)
Mars	142,000,000 miles (229,000,000 km)
Jupiter	484,000,000 miles (779,000,000 km)
Saturn	886,000,000 miles (1,427,000,000 km)
Uranus	1,784,000,000 miles (2,871,000,000 km)
Neptune	2,795,000,000 miles (4,498,000,000 km)

GLOSSARY

atmosphere: the mixture of gases that surround a planet

data: facts and figures

gravity: the force that pulls objects toward the center of a planet or star

million: 1,000 thousand, or 1,000,000

NASA: stands for the National Aeronautics and Space Administration, the part of the U.S. government in charge of space study and exploration

spacecraft: a vehicle used for traveling into space

support: to provide something that's needed

surface: the top layer of a planet

telescope: a tool that makes faraway objects look bigger and closer

temperature: how hot or cold something is

volcano: an opening in a planet's surface through which hot, liquid rock sometimes flows

FOR MORE INFORMATION

BOOKS

Gillespie, Katie. *Planets*. New York, NY: AV2 By Weigl, 2018.

Jankeliowitch, Anne. *Solar System*. Cambridge, MA: Barefoot Books, 2019.

WEBSITES

All About the Planets
spaceplace.nasa.gov/planets/en/
Learn about the planets on this fun site.

What Is an Exoplanet?
spaceplace.nasa.gov/all-about-exoplanets/en/
Discover how scientists find exoplanets.

Publisher's note to educators and parents: Our editors have carefully reviewed this website to ensure that it is suitable for students. Many websites change frequently, however, and we cannot guarantee that a site's future contents will continue to meet our high standards of quality and educational value. Be advised that students should be closely supervised whenever they access the internet.

INDEX